# DO TARANTULAS HAVE TEETH?

## Questions and Answers About Poisonous Creatures

BY MELVIN AND GILDA BERGER
ILLUSTRATED BY JIM EFFLER

SCHOLASTIC REFERENCE

# CONTENTS

**KEY TO ABBREVIATIONS**
cm = centimeter/centimetre
cm² = square centimeter/centimetre
km = kilometer/kilometre
l = liter
m = meter/metre
t = tonne

Text copyright © 1999 by Melvin Berger and Gilda Berger
Illustrations © 1999 by Jim Effler

*Library of Congress Cataloging-in-Publication Data*

Berger, Melvin.
   Do tarantulas have teeth?: questions and answers about poisonous creatures / by Melvin Berger and Gilda Berger; illustrated by Jim Effler.
      p.    cm.—(Scholastic question and answer series)
   Includes index.
   Summary: Provides answers to a variety of questions about various poisonous creatures, such as "Do Gila monsters bite humans?", "What are killer bees?", "Which ant sting hurts the most?", and "Are frogs poisonous?"
   1. Poisonous animals—Miscellanea—Juvenile literature.  [1. Poisonous animals—Miscellanea.  2. Questions and answers.]  I. Berger, Gilda.  II. Effler, James M., 1956– ill.  III. Title.  IV. Series: Berger, Melvin.  Scholastic questions and answer series.
   QL 100.B47   1999   591.6'5—dc21   99-17402   CIP   AC

ISBN 0-439-09578-6 (pob); ISBN 0-439-14877-4 (pb)

*Book design by David Saylor and Nancy Sabato*

      14  15                    5 6 / 0

Printed in the U.S.A.   08
First trade printing, September 2000

Expert reader: Anthony P. Brownie, Wildlife Conservation Society, Central Park Wildlife Center, New York, NY

*The poisonous creature on the cover is a Mexican red knee tarantula.*

For Jacob Leary, a wonderful guy
with an inquiring mind
— M. AND G. BERGER

To Dad, who took me camping when I was young,
sparking an interest in nature
— J. EFFLER

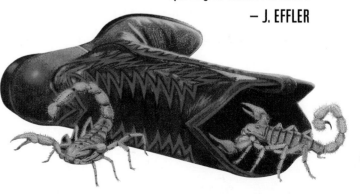

## Which is the largest poisonous animal in the world?

The king cobra. This huge snake can grow to a length of 18 feet (5.5 m)—longer than a pickup truck. When threatened, it raises its head up to 4 feet (1.2 m) off the ground. Then it strikes its prey.

The cobra then usually hangs on. It chews the venom deep into the wound, driving more and more of the poison into the victim's flesh. One bite has enough venom to kill an elephant. In fact, the king cobra is the only creature in the wild that elephants fear.

## Do spitting cobras really spit?

No. Spitting cobras squirt. The deadly venom shoots out of holes near the tips of their fangs, like water from a water pistol. These 6-foot (2 m) snakes can squirt six times before using up their supply of venom. They have perfect aim up to nearly 8 feet (2.4 m).

Scientists think that the snakes aim at shiny objects. In most victims, this is the eyes. The venom can blind. Then the spitting cobra bites like other cobras. A tiny fraction of an ounce (gram) of venom is enough to kill 165 humans or 160,000 mice.

## Did poisonous snakes ever win a war?

Yes. The great general Hannibal (247–183 B.C.) once used live snakes to win a war. He threw jars of venomous snakes onto the decks of enemy ships. The poisonous creatures frightened the sailors so much that they surrendered without a fight!

## Can a small mongoose kill a big cobra?

Yes. In Rudyard Kipling's *The Jungle Book*, an Indian mongoose kills two cobras. That make-believe mongoose wasn't just very lucky. Even in real fights, the small, swift mongoose is one of the few animals able to avoid the poisonous bite of the slow-moving cobra. Unless, of course, the mongoose is slow and careless, and the cobra is fast and deadly.

# Which snakes look like twins?

The milk snake and the coral snake. Both have bright red, yellow, and black rings. But only the coral snake has the red ring touching the yellow. Animals that have learned to stay away from the poisonous coral snake also avoid the harmless milk snake.

But don't let these two snakes fool you. Use this rhyme to help you figure out which is which:

> *Red touch yellow,*
> *Bad for a fellow,*
> *Red touch black,*
> *Good for Jack.*

Even if your name's not Jack, "red touch black" is the safe milk snake.

Louisiana milk snake

## How can you tell a poisonous snake from a nonpoisonous snake?

Most times you can't. The rattlesnake, for example, looks much like the nonpoisonous water snake. The poisonous copperhead and the nonpoisonous corn snake are also look-alikes. All have triangular heads, narrow necks, stout bodies, and short tails. Yet not all poisonous snakes have these features. Nor do harmless snakes always resemble their poisonous cousins.

So—it's best to avoid all snakes. Never try to catch or kill a snake. Never pick up a snake, dead or alive. And if you are bitten, see a doctor right away.

## Can doctors treat snakebites?

Yes. Doctors have special medicines—called antivenins—that fight the snake poison in the human body.

You may be surprised to learn that snake poison sometimes helps fight other human illnesses. Medicine made from the venom of a Russell's viper helps blood to clot. And poison from the Malaysian pit viper stops blood from clotting and prevents unwanted blood clots from forming inside the body.

Many Chinese folk remedies use snake blood. It is thought to help the liver and lungs. It surely doesn't help the thousands of snakes killed each year for this purpose!

Arizona coral snake

## Do any snakes live in the ocean?

Sea snakes do. And they are killers. Sea snakes are about 100 times more deadly than the most poisonous land snakes! Sea snakes are found only in tropical waters. They prey mostly on eels, which they kill with bites along the body.

People can die from sea snake bites, too, especially if they make the mistake of picking up a sea snake while fishing. Even a very small bite can kill.

## Which is the most poisonous creature in the sea?

The puffer fish. When eaten, the deadly poison in its body can kill.

Many Japanese people love the taste of the puffer fish, which they call *fugu*. Often, they will pay large sums for meals of *fugu* prepared by chefs trained in the proper way to remove the poison parts from the animal. Still, accidents do happen. For about 30 people a year, a dinner of puffer fish is the last meal of their lives.

The puffer fish got its name because it blows itself up to the size of a soccer ball when it senses danger.

## Which tiny sea creature kills more people than any shark?

The blue-ringed octopus. Usually, it preys on crabs and small fish in the waters off Australia, biting them with a dose of poison before eating them. Its venom is the same poison found in the puffer fish.

Every so often a swimmer picks up the very pretty little animal for a closer look. That's when the blue-ringed octopus bites hard with its parrot-like beak. A powerful poison—more deadly than any shark—spurts into the wound.

The blue-ringed octopus is only $1^{1}/_{4}$ inch (3 cm) long, bigger than a silver dollar. But it can bite and kill anyone who picks it up. The poison of this sea creature is more deadly than that of any land animal.

Puffer fish

Gila monster

## How many lizards are poisonous?

Only 2 of the 3,000 different kinds of lizards. Of these, the almost 20-inch (50 cm) Gila (HEE-luh) monster is best known. Tough and rugged, it lives in the hot desert regions of the southwestern United States. Its bright blotches of color—pink, orange, or white on black—warn enemies away.

The Gila monster is named after the Gila River in Arizona. The other poisonous lizard is the similar-looking beaded lizard of Mexico.

## How does the Gila monster kill?

It bites with its fangs. The Gila monster has a large head with poison glands at the back of its jaw. Ducts in its grooved teeth deliver the poison. This lizard preys on nesting birds and baby animals. When it is about to bite, its teeth fill up with poison. Like the tarantula, the Gila monster chews poison into the wound.

The Gila monster usually moves very slowly. But when it spots its prey or a fearsome enemy, it swings into action. Sometimes the Gila monster will hold on to its victim for as long as 10 minutes. By then the poison has killed the animal. The Gila monster may not be quick, but it sure is stubborn!

## Do Gila monsters bite humans?

Almost never in the wild—but sometimes when caged or roughly handled. When a Gila monster attacks, it's usually for a good reason. A zoo visitor once teased a Gila monster with his bare hand. The lizard bit hard. Its venom caused terrible pain, swelling, and heavy sweating. Fortunately the person got better. But one thing is sure: He never bothered a Gila monster again.

# ANIMALS THAT STING

## Which poisonous creatures have the deadliest stingers?

Honeybees. They kill about as many people in the United States each year as all venomous snakes put together.

The honeybee's stinger is at the rear end of its body. The stinger, much smaller than a fang, has barbs, or hooks, along its sides. Most of the time the stinger is hidden, yet ready for quick use if needed. Honey may be sweet—but the honeybee isn't!

## Do all honeybees sting?

Most, but not all. A honeybee colony has up to 60,000 bees. It includes one female queen bee, a few hundred male drone bees, and thousands of female worker bees. Only the worker bees sting.

The queen bee also has a stinger. But she uses it only to sting another queen bee. She never uses it on worker drones or people. Also, her stinger is smooth, not barbed like other bees' stingers. Unlike all other bees, she can sting over and over.

## Why do honeybees sting?

Usually to protect their colony. Honeybees only sting if animals disturb them or come too close to their nest. That's because they do not prey on animals. Their normal diet is the nectar and pollen of flowers.

Honeybee venom is not very strong and the reaction in humans may be mild. There's a little pain and some swelling where the bee stings, but soon it is all gone.

The real danger is to people with allergies. One or more stings can interfere with their breathing and cause severe swelling. A person allergic to bee stings may even die.

Honeybees

Killer bee

## Can a honeybee sting more than once?

It all depends. Suppose the honeybee stings an animal, such as a mouse, a bear, or a person. Then it can sting only once. The barbs hold the stinger in place. As the bee flies away, its stinger and poison gland rip out of its body. The bee dies within one hour. But the gland is still stuck in the victim's wound, pumping poison.

But suppose the bee stings a small insect. The bee does not lose its stinger. It can use it to sting again and again and again.

## What are killer bees?

A nervous, quicker-to-sting kind of honeybee. Killer bees are a little smaller than honeybees and fly a little faster. Because they are from Africa, killer bees are also called African honeybees.

## Do killer bees have stronger poison than honeybees?

No. Nor do killer bees have bigger stingers. But they are more dangerous than their honeybee cousins, which is how they got their name.

Killer bees rush to attack anything that approaches their nest. They stop at nothing. If the victim tries to flee, the killer bees will follow for up to 1 mile (1.6 km), flying as fast as 12 miles (19.3 km) an hour. That is faster than most humans can run! And not one, but a swarm of killer bees goes after any animal or person that disturbs them.

## How should you treat a bee sting?

Scratch the site with a fingernail to get the stinger out. Don't grab the stinger and pull on it! The stinger is still attached to the poison gland. Pulling it will force more poison into your body.

Once the stinger is out, wash the area with soap and water. Use an ice pack to ease the pain. If you don't feel better soon, see a doctor.

## Are bumblebees as poisonous as honeybees?

Yes. But bumblebees cause far less harm. Bumblebees can be as much as three times the size of honeybees. Yet they are much gentler. They are also fewer in number.

The bumblebee stinger does not have barbs. The bee can pull out its stinger and sting again. The sting is painful and leaves a red mark, but rarely hurts for long.

## How can you tell a bumblebee from a yellow jacket wasp?

With difficulty. Bumblebees and yellow jackets both have yellow-and-black bodies. The bodies of most wasps are smooth, while bees generally are hairy. Female wasps and female bees have stingers on their rear end. And both mainly feed on the nectar of flowers. But wasps also attack bigger animals. A few kinds even kill and eat caterpillars and spiders.

## Can wasps sting more than once?

Yes. Wasps have smooth stingers without barbs. They can pull the stinger out of the victim and sting more than once. Any animal or person unlucky enough to disturb a wasp's nest had better take cover. The individual will soon be set upon by a swarm of angry wasps, each one stinging again and again. Wasp stings are sharp and painful. In most cases, there is some swelling.

## What makes female wasps good mothers?

They catch insects for their young to eat. The female wasp first stings the insect. The poison paralyzes the bug, making it unable to move.

Some wasps then eat the insect and spit it up to feed their young. Others put the paralyzed insect in their nest, and then lay an egg on it. Later, when the young wasp hatches, it finds its first meal ready and waiting thanks to its good mother.

Yellow jacket

Bumblebee

Digger wasp

## Who would win a battle between a digger wasp and a tarantula?

No contest. The much smaller wasp almost always wins over the bigger tarantula. The female digger wasp is able to quickly sting and paralyze the tarantula. Then the wasp drags the spider to her nest, which is usually a hole in the ground. She covers the unmoving tarantula with dirt. She leaves it there for her young wasps to eat after they hatch.

## Why is one kind of wasp called a velvet ant?

Because it looks more like an ant than a wasp. Unlike other wasps, the female velvet ant has a big, brushlike, bright red or orange growth on its back and no wings.

Velvet ants have some of the longest stingers in the wasp family. The stingers are also very sharp and contain a very powerful venom. Mostly these wasps attack solitary bees or other wasps. But they can also give humans stings they long remember.

## Were wasps ever used to kill prisoners?

Yes, in ancient Rome. A favorite punishment was death by stinging.

The prisoner was first covered with honey and tied up near a hive of angry wasps. The wasps knew what to do. They went for the honey and ended up stinging the prisoner to death.

## How can you avoid getting stung by a wasp?

Never touch or disturb a wasp's nest. Don't reach into fallen logs or dark corners of sheds or barns where wasps like to make their homes. Avoid using fragrant lotion, hair spray, or deodorant when you're going on a hike or a picnic, since the smells attract and excite wasps. Finally, cover up as much as you can with long-sleeved shirts, trousers, and shoes with socks.

## Are ants poisonous creatures?

A few are. Poisonous ants have venom glands and stingers at the end of their bodies. Don't get mixed up. Many kinds of ants have stingers—but without poison. Of course, these ants are harmless.

## Which ant sting hurts the most?

The sting of the fire ant. This bug may be tiny, but it packs a big one-two punch. First it clamps its powerful jaws deep in the victim's flesh. Then, while holding on tightly, the ant injects a dose of venom. The sting burns like the touch of a red-hot needle.

Even then, the ant is not done. Keeping its jaws locked in place, the fire ant wiggles its rear end and stings again in a different place. Wiggle and sting, wiggle and sting, wiggle and sting. Before long a small circle of bright red sting marks surround the central bite mark.

## Which poisonous ant do people fear most?

The bulldog ant of Australia. Everything about this creature spells trouble.

Bulldog ants are large—up to 1 inch (2.5 cm) long. Their poison is also very strong. Since they live in large colonies, bulldog ants attack in huge numbers. And like bulldogs, they just don't let go.

Bulldog ants sting animals or people who even come close to their nest. I'd keep my distance, wouldn't you?

## Can ants put out a fire?

Perhaps. In 1930, scientist Marguerite Combs dropped a lighted match near a colony of ants. As she watched, the ants rushed out and squirted poison at the flames. After they put out the fire, the ants left.

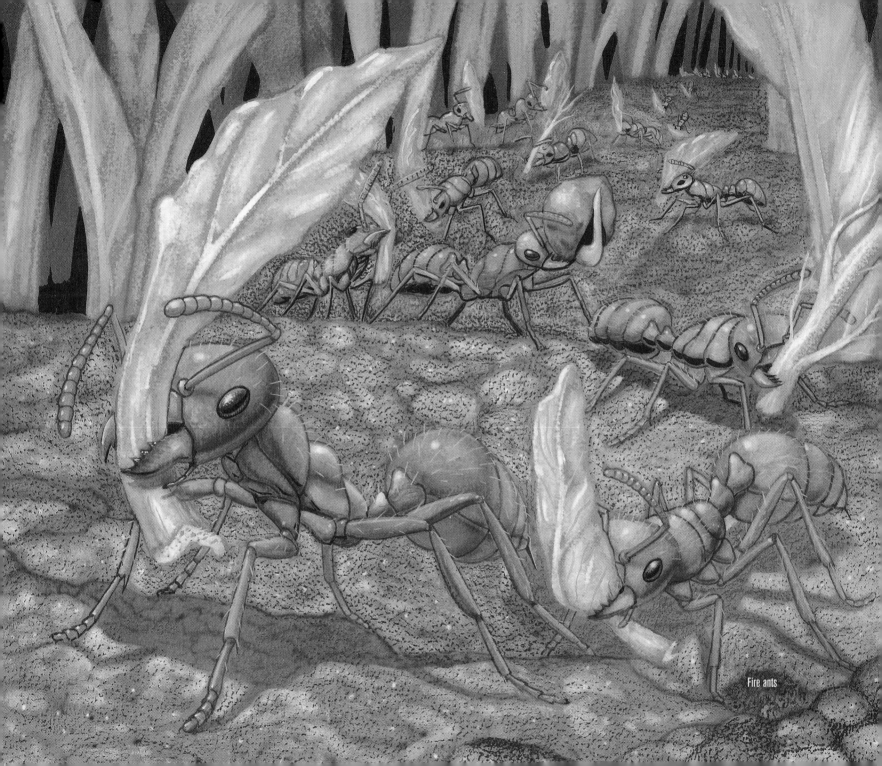
Fire ants

Scorpions

## What do scorpions look like?

Like tiny lobsters. And like lobsters, scorpions have eight legs, plus two large claws up front. There the similarity ends!

## How does a scorpion sting?

With a special stinger on its tail. At the back of the scorpion's body is a tail that arches, or curls up, over its body. Sticking out from the end of the tail is the mean-looking, poisonous stinger. When attacking, the scorpion whips its stinger forward in a millisecond!

## Which animals are prey for scorpions?

Insects, spiders, frogs, and mice. The scorpion grabs the animal with its claws. Quickly flipping its stinger over its head, the scorpion injects a shot of poison. Then the scorpion tears the victim apart. At the same time, it covers the animal's body with saliva. Chemicals in the saliva start to digest the flesh. Finally, the scorpion sucks up the mushy body.

A large animal or person that comes too close will alarm the scorpion and become a target for its poison. Scorpion stings hurt but do not usually kill humans. Only one kind of scorpion is very dangerous. It lives in Brazil and kills more than 100 people a year.

## Why do cowboys sometimes sleep with their boots on?

Because they're afraid of scorpions. Many poisonous scorpions live in the hot, dry regions of the southwestern United States where cowboys work.

Scorpions hunt at night and hide during the day. Unfortunately, they love warm, dark places—like the insides of boots. The way cowboys figure it—it's better to sleep with their boots on than to get a nasty surprise the next morning. Why take chances?

# Do any sea creatures sting?

Jellyfish do. Long, stringy tentacles hang down from their floating bodies. The tentacles are covered with poisonous nerve cells. Each cell is packed with a long, sharp, poison-covered thread.

When an enemy or something good to eat touches a tentacle, the nerve cells explode. Poisoned threads shoot out and paralyze the victim. With its tentacles, the jellyfish slowly brings its dinner to its mouth.

If you're unlucky enough to touch a jellyfish, the sting will burn and itch. Just remember to rub the spot with salt water. It will help to put out the "fire."

# Which is the most poisonous jellyfish?

The sea wasp, or box jellyfish. This poisonous creature looks like a cantaloupe floating on the water. It is about 10 inches (25 cm) across. Hanging down from its body are about 60 tentacles, each one about 20 feet (6 m) long. Mostly found in the waters off the coasts of Australia and southeast Asia, the sea wasp scares swimmers and divers. Its stinging tentacles can kill a person in two to three minutes.

# What makes the sea wasp so dangerous?

Its tentacles are covered with about one-half million nerve cells in every square inch (6.2 cm²)! That's like 500,000 loaded cannons waiting to be fired!

Sea wasp poison is superpowerful. The tentacles of a single sea wasp hold enough poison to kill 60 people. A person could die from brushing against just half the length of a single tentacle.

# Do sea wasps have a brain?

No. Sea wasps have no brain, no bones, no shell, and no skin. All they have is an excellent way to get food and kill attackers. It seems that's quite enough!

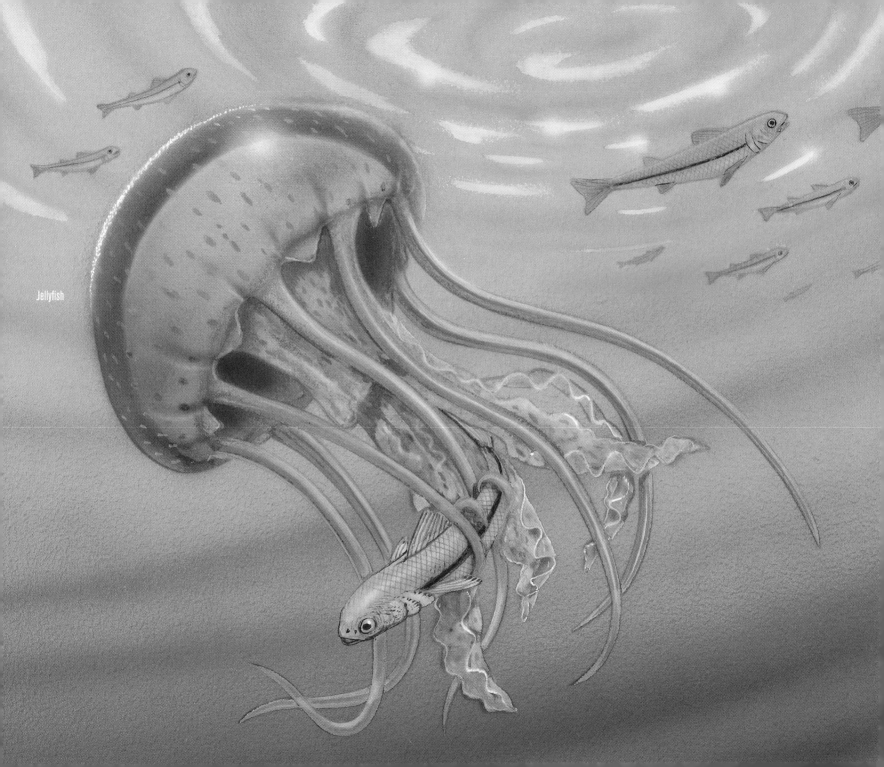

Jellyfish

## Is the Portuguese man-of-war a jellyfish?

Yes and no. The Portuguese man-of-war is related to the jellyfish. But it is not a single animal. The Portuguese man-of-war is a colony of tiny creatures living together as one. Beneath its body float deadly stinging tentacles loaded with poison "harpoons." Each tentacle can be more than 30 feet (15 m) long.

Wind and currents move the large blue body of the Portuguese man-of-war across the water. One Portuguese man-of-war can kill more than 20 fish at a time!

## Which sea creature looks like a flower, but poisons like a jellyfish?

The sea anemone (SEE uh-NEM-uh-nee). It grows on rocks at the bottom of the ocean. Instead of leaves, the sea anemone has poisonous tentacles that sway back and forth in the moving water. And just like a jellyfish, the sea anemone kills and eats small sea creatures that happen to swim by.

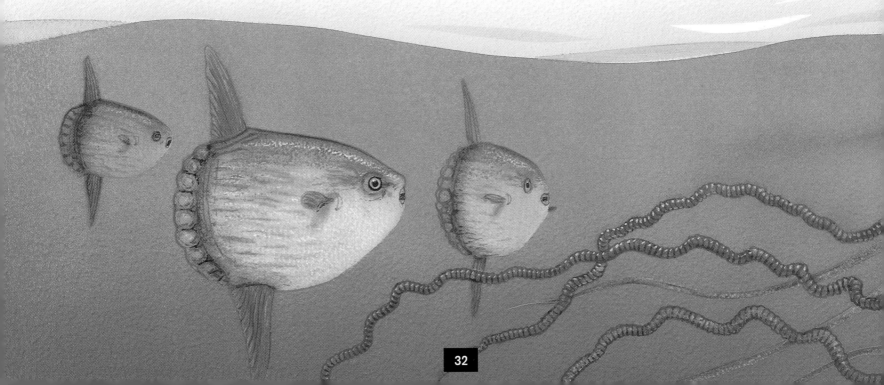

# Are any fish safe around the Portuguese man-of-war and the sea anemone?

Yes. Some fish are immune to their poisons. Ocean sunfishes are safe around the Portuguese man-of-war; clown fishes live happily among the tentacles of the sea anemone. But other fish get stung as soon as they approach either of these poisonous creatures. The victims include enemies of sunfishes and clown fishes.

In return for protection, the ocean sunfish helps to keep the Portuguese man-of-war clean. The clown fish shares the fish it attracts with the sea anemone.

Portuguese man-of-war

# ANIMALS DANGEROUS TO TOUCH

## Are frogs poisonous?

Yes, most are. Frogs, and toads, too, have special glands that make strong poisons. They use this poison to defend themselves from enemies, not to capture prey.

When they are scared or excited, poison oozes out onto their skin. Some poisons are strong enough to harm other animals. The poison burns the mouth of any animal that tries to eat the frog. In a few cases, the poison is powerful enough to kill.

A kiss may change a frog into a prince in a fairy tale. But it's not something you want to try in real life!

## What do poisonous frogs look like?

They are usually brightly colored. The coloring warns the frog's enemies to stay away.

Sometimes a snake or bird grabs a poisonous frog with its mouth. The frog's poison burns and numbs. This teaches the enemy a lesson: Never touch a brightly colored frog!

## Which frog has the strongest poison?

The poison arrow frog, sometimes called the poison dart frog. Most poison arrow frogs have bright patterns of red, black, yellow, green, or blue. They're usually found in the tropical rain forests of South and Central America.

People look out for this moist, slippery, and rather small frog, which is about the length of your thumb. A single drop of the very powerful venom from a poison arrow frog could kill more than 1,000 people.

American toad

Poison arrow frog

## How do native people use the poison from poison arrow frogs?

For hunting animals in the rain forest. Some hunters dip darts in the venom from poison arrow frogs. They put the darts into a blowgun and shoot them at their prey. When a dart strikes a monkey or a jaguar, the hunter follows the animal and waits for it to collapse and die.

Rain forest hunters have many ways to remove the poison from the frogs. One way is to roast them on sticks over a hot fire. The hunters collect the poison that drips out of the frogs' skin and rub it on their darts. One frog supplies enough poison for 50 darts.

## How did ancient Romans use the poison from toads?

For murder! Two thousand years ago, Romans used the poison from toads to kill their enemies. A person who got a mouthful of poison might die in an hour.

At that time, someone wrote that "crushed frogs soaked in wine are good against the poisoning of toads." We guess that recipe was used when the murderer had a change of heart!

Poison arrow frog

## What happens if someone steps on a stingray?

Plenty. Stingrays are large, flat fish with long tails. They lie buried in sand on the ocean bottom. Sticking up from their tails are one or more long, stiff, sharp spines. When a person steps on, or even touches, the spine of the stingray it immediately injects the victim with a powerful dose of poison. The Romans used the stings to treat toothaches. That's one way to take someone's mind off his or her troubles!

## What sea creature is more dangerous than the stingray?

The stonefish. This dark, wart-covered fish spends most of its time on the ocean floor looking like a rock. On its back are about one dozen needlelike spines. The spines are sharp and strong enough to cut through flippers or sneakers. The pain is horrible. If untreated, the wound may become infected by the very strong poison, and the person may lose the limb.

## Which poisonous sea creatures are very brightly colored?

Scorpion fishes, a group of fish that includes lionfish, zebra fish, and turkey fish. All are armed with dangerous poisonous spines.

An enemy that bites a scorpion fish and lives learns never to bite that kind of fish again. So, like other poisonous creatures, the flashy colors of the scorpion fish warn of danger. "Keep away," they signal, loud and clear!

## How do sea snails kill?

With a long, ribbonlike tongue covered with dart-shaped teeth. A sea snail, also called a cone shell, sticks its tongue out at its prey, which may be a worm or a small fish. It then shoots out a tiny harpoon that spears the animal and keeps it still. Last, it injects its prey with powerful poison.

Stingrays

Io moth
caterpillar

Flannel moth
caterpillar

Saddleback
caterpillar

# How do some caterpillars protect themselves?

With poisonous needlelike spines over all or part of their body. A caterpillar is the second stage in the life of a butterfly or a moth. At this stage, the insects are small and slow-moving. They lack claws or fangs to fight back. And they have many, many enemies, including birds and other insects.

The poisonous spines offer caterpillars some protection. But even so, the death rate is very high. Few caterpillars live long enough to become butterflies or moths.

# Which caterpillars are poisonous?

The caterpillars of the Malay lacewing butterfly, for example. At the base of each spine is a tiny gland that emits poison. The poison passes through the hair and onto any predator that touches the caterpillar. The pain that comes from touching the hair often saves the caterpillar from becoming lunch for its attacker.

# Which is the most poisonous caterpillar?

The caterpillar of the brown flannel moth. This caterpillar is completely covered with poisonous hairs. Just brushing against it can give a person painful blisters and a rash that lasts for a week.

The caterpillars of the io moth and saddleback moth are also very dangerous. Their spines are both poisonous and painful.

# Which moth uses poison to win its mate?

The male bella moth. In the caterpillar stage, it eats poisonous seeds that make it poisonous. The seeds also give the adult moth a certain scent. The males that eat the greatest number of seeds have the strongest smell. They're the ones that get the females of their dreams!

## What makes some butterflies poisonous?

The poisonous plants they eat. The monarch butterfly is a good example of a poisonous butterfly. It eats milkweed, a plant containing a poison that makes some animals sick. Birds that try to eat the monarch butterfly taste the poison. Ugh! They spit it out in a hurry and usually learn to leave the butterfly alone.

Birds also stay away from the viceroy butterfly. The viceroy is not poisonous. But it is a monarch look-alike. That's enough to send birds looking for something else to eat.

## How does the garden tiger moth fight off its enemies?

With its disgusting smell! When threatened by one of its enemies—a spider, bird, frog, or lizard—the garden tiger moth forms small, bad-smelling bubbles on its body. Few animals want to go near an insect with an odor so vile. Would you?

## Which beetles spray their attackers with poisonous fluid?

Bombardier beetles. These tiny, bright-blue-and-orange bugs are barely larger than the ants that sometimes attack them. Yet small as they are, bombardier beetles can defend themselves very well.

The beetle prepares for battle by squeezing chemicals in its body into a boiling-hot poison. When an attacker approaches, the beetle sprays the powerful gas at its face. The beetle's aim is perfect. It can hit targets in any direction.

## How did the bombardier beetle get its name?

From the exploding sounds it makes when spraying its attackers. The sounds are like little popguns going off one after another. Sometimes four or five of these "bombs" go off in quick order. The explosion creates a noise you can actually hear.

Bombardier beetles

Ladybugs

## What does the darkling beetle do when touched?

It stands on its head! And, just like the bombardier beetle, it sprays a poisonous liquid at its enemy.

But the darkling has a problem. It's slower than the bombardier beetle. Before it can let loose with its spray, the darkling is often grabbed by its worst enemy, the grasshopper mouse. The mouse shoves the beetle's rear end into the ground! What use is the darkling's poison in that position?

## Which beetles shoot poison from their knees?

Ladybugs, which are a kind of beetle. The poison is blood that spurts from their knee joints when they are attacked. Believe it or not, the ladybug's blood is yellow, not red! And it's smelly enough to scare away enemies and irritate sensitive skin.

## How did stink bugs get their name?

That's easy. Stink bugs smell bad! Their dazzling colors and bold designs alert enemies to their poisonous power. The bad smell comes from glands between their middle and hind legs.

## Do millipedes fight with chemicals?

Some do. When disturbed, some millipedes produce nasty poison. The poison comes out from a row of glands along their sides. Scientists think that the poison can blind a small animal. If it lands on a person it can cause a rash.

One African millipede drenches its attackers in deadly clouds of poisonous gas. When touched, this millipede shoots out puffs of gas from both sides of its body at the same time. The word *millipede* means "thousand-foot." But millipedes have only between 20 and several hundred feet. The record-setter had 710 feet!

## Are any mammals poisonous?

The ratlike American short-tailed shrew. These mammals have poisonous saliva that paralyzes the frogs and fish they eat. Scientists have found that one short-tailed shrew produces enough poison in its venom gland to kill 200 fish!

## Which mammal has a poisonous kick?

The duck-billed platypus of Australia. The males have poisonous spurs on their hind ankles. One scratch from a spur can kill a dog or cause a human severe pain.

No one is sure of the real purpose of the poisonous spurs. Some think platypuses use the poison to stab other males in fights over females. Others say the spurs are used on the spur of the moment!

## Are any birds poisonous?

Until 1991 no one thought so. Then a scientist handled the pitohui bird of New Guinea. His hands burned and grew numb. The news startled everyone. The pitohui bird was the first poisonous bird known to humans. Its poison is much like that of the poison arrow frog. Oddly enough, the frog and bird also look somewhat alike with their orange and black colors.

## Do any poisonous creatures prey on humans?

No. Humans are not the main target of any poisonous creature in the world.

Still, the poison of many kinds of animals can harm you. But don't be afraid. Learn about the habits and markings of poisonous creatures. Then use common sense and be careful when you explore outdoors. Do not annoy or pick up unfamiliar animals. That way you can live in peace with poisonous creatures almost anywhere you go.

Short-tailed shrews

# INDEX

## About the Authors

"Between us," say the Bergers, "we have been bitten by spiders, stung by honeybees, and touched by jellyfish. Thankfully, most of what we know about tarantulas, rattlesnakes, Gila monsters, and stingrays comes from research. Our work on this book has taught us never to eat a puffer fish, pick up a blue-ringed octopus, or kiss a brightly colored frog!"

## About the Illustrator

Jim Effler has been drawing since he was two years old. That was 41 years ago! He enjoys looking for details in natural things. Jim lives in Cincinnati with his wife, Debbie, and his daughters, Jenna and Ariana.